A Boy Named Rocky

A Boy Named Rocky

a coloring book for the children of incarcerated parents

Illustrations by: Cale E. Carter

Dr. Janice Beal, Judge Vanessa Gilmore

To order additional copies of this book, contact:
Xlibris
844-714-8691
www.Xlibris.com
Orders@Xlibris.com
824289

Dedicated to
our children

Jasmine

&

Sean

For The Parent, Guardian, or Psychotherapist:

Children with incarcerated parents are an invisible population. There is no one agency that is responsible for them and their welfare. Nationwide, more than 2 million children have a parent who is incarcerated in state and federal prisons, and local jails (U.S. Department of Justice 2007). Since 1991, the number has continued to increase by more than 50%. About one child in 40 had an incarcerated father in 1998, while one child in 360 had an incarcerated mother (BJS 2000). Currently, 1 in 142 adults in the United States is in prison or jail (Lee 2007). The female inmate population had more than tripled since 1985. When a parent leaves the home, the majority of the children will be placed with a relative, while others will end up in the child welfare system.

Research on children of incarcerated parents indicates that the loss of a parental figure, especially the mother, has a profound effect on minor children and adolescents. Children retain bonds and love for parents regardless of the label attached to them by society. One study estimated that children with imprisoned parents are almost six times more likely than their peers to become criminally involved and incarcerated at some point in their lives.

Children who are separated from their parents by incarceration can have a variety of strong emotions exacerbated by this family situation, including anger, isolation/sadness, fear/anxiety and guilt. These emotions and their reactions to them can lead to problems or violence, erosion of self-esteem and "risky" or dysfunctional behaviors. Many of these children see no chance of having their lives follow paths which are any different from their parents. This coloring book was designed to help the child discuss and understand their feelings. It can be used in several therapeutic settings to explore loss and create treatment plans for the minor child.

Janice M. Beal, Ed.D.
Clinical Director
Beal Counseling Associates

FOREWORD

Collateral damage is a term that originated with the U.S. military to describe unintentional or incidental injury or damage during times of war to persons who are not actually military targets. In the "War On Drugs" and other criminal justice initiatives, the children of the incarcerated have become the unintended victims. Just as the innocent military victims are left hurt, angry and damaged so are the children of the incarcerated. Unlike their military counterparts, however, the children of the incarcerated are almost always left to suffer in poverty with no sense of obligation by the government to address their unintended injuries.

The military has gone to great lengths to minimize collateral damage, but the same cannot always be said for the criminal justice system. Although there are programs to assure that mothers who are pregnant at the time they are incarcerated will have some time to bond with their infants, those programs generally require the mother to make arrangements to turn the child over to a family member or state agency within a relatively short time after they deliver. After that, there generally are no formal programs designed to maintain or encourage the parental relationship.

Although not much attention is devoted to the feelings of the parents who are facing incarceration, my twenty-seven years on the bench have shown me that these parents feel significant pain, remorse and regret about the impact that their incarceration will have on their children. Sadly, their children are acutely aware of their circumstances and often write to judges to implore them to spare their parent and send them home. While well meaning, this often adds to the shame and humiliation that the parents face and to the sense of hopelessness of the children who are unable to save their parents. Most parents, however, long for the opportunity to stay connected to their families during incarceration and will often seek placement in an institution that is located close enough to allow their families to visit them on a regular basis. Sometimes this is possible, but often it is not and in those instances, the distance puts more strain on an already fragile relationship.

One of the things that this coloring book is designed to do is encourage what some have referred to as the "lost art of letter writing" as a means of maintaining the connection between incarcerated parents and their children. While prisoners can make phone calls from prison, they must usually be made as collect calls and are very expensive. The benefit of letter writing by children are too numerous to count, but for the children of incarcerated parents, it can also provide an invaluable connection between parent and child that would be impossible to attain any other way. Maintaining the family connection is important for the incarcerated as they contemplate their futures and reintegrate themselves into their communities. A strong family connection can play an important role in preventing recidivism upon release and it is the hope of the authors that this publication will provide positive steps in that direction.

Vanessa D. Gilmore
United States District Judge (retired)

This is a story about a little boy named James. His friends and family call him "Rocky." Rocky was nicknamed when he was three years old because he would always carry rocks in his pockets. At night when his mother helped him undress for bed, she would fondly say, "Come here, my little "Rocky" and let's unload your pockets."

Rocky remembered all of the good times he and his mother shared before his family began to have problems. Rocky's father left home one day when Rocky was five years old and never returned. They had to move from their home into an apartment to save money. Life, as he knew it, began to change.

At first his mom was doing okay, but he could tell it was hard for her to pay the bills. At night instead of tucking him into bed, she just sat at the kitchen table crying, and sometimes she drank alcohol. Rocky would try to help, but things only got worse. He noticed that his mother's behavior changed. She stopped cooking, cleaning, and putting on makeup. Sometimes she even hit him for no reason. He didn't tell anyone, not even Grandma Jackson how bad things were at home.

One day when he returned home from school, there was a note on the door that said to call grandma. When Grandma Jackson came, she told him that he would be living with her for a while. Rocky became scared because he didn't know what to expect. "Where is my mom? What happened to her?"

He could see the tears in grandma's eyes. Grandma Jackson explained that his mom was stopped by the police earlier that day for selling and using drugs. She was incarcerated. Rocky looked puzzled as he asked, "What's incarcerated? Will I see her again? Is she alright?"

Grandma Jackson said that it meant she was in jail. Rocky suddenly remembered other kids in his neighborhood talking about their dads being in jail, but never anyone's mom. "How long will she be gone?", he asked. Grandma didn't know the answer.

The next couple of months were hard for Rocky. He would feel happy, sad, and angry, all at the same time. Rocky had a hard time adjusting to losing his mother. He mostly felt confused. He could not be happy if she was locked up.

Grandma would take him to visit his mom which made him feel worse instead of better. They talked about how he was doing, and he would always say "I'm okay," but that was not how he really felt inside.

Rocky's grades dropped in school. He would sit outside and cry but he didn't want anyone to know. He was angry with his mom, his dad, himself, and the whole world. He began to blame himself for everything that had gone wrong in his family.

Some days he skipped school. He would wait until Grandma Jackson turned the corner then run down the street. Once he even thought about selling drugs when a teenager on the street corner offered them to him. He was told that he could make a lot of money and help his family.

Mrs. Matthews, Rocky's teacher, noticed the change in his behavior and called the school counselor. Together they called his grandmother. Grandma Jackson went to the school for a meeting, and the counselor shared information with her about a group led by Dr. Brown, a psychologist. This group was for children of incarcerated parents.

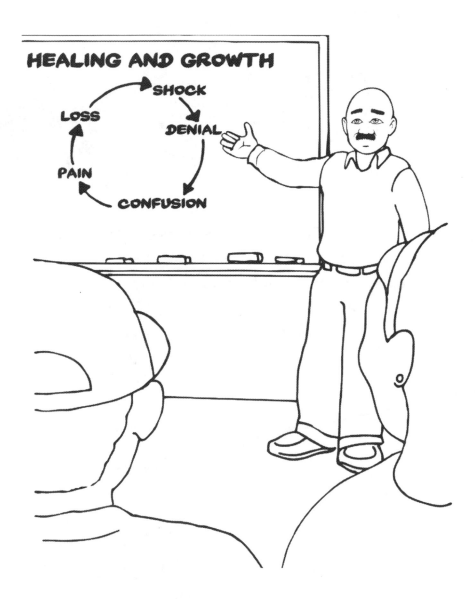

Dr. Brown talked with kids Rocky's age about grief. He said, "When you lose someone, whether they are taken away through death, divorce, incarceration, or if they decide to leave on their own, it brings about a change in how you feel. Most people feel sad. This change is called grief. The hurt and pain of grief comes and goes. There will be ups and downs." Dr. Brown even drew a picture on the board.

He said the best way to handle these emotions is to talk about how you are feeling in order to keep things from exploding inside. Rocky would go to the group once a week. Sometimes he and his grandmother would meet with Dr. Brown. Counseling helped him to understand his mother being gone and to express his feelings. He later found out that his mother was also seeing a counselor. Rocky began to feel better about himself.

Dear Rocky,

I love you so much, and I am sorry we are apart. If I had to do it all over again, I would not do anyting to separate us. I just did not know how to make good choices. Don't do what I did. Always stop and think about the consequences of your actions. Talk about your feelings, don't keep things inside. Stay on the right path. Do what your teachers and grandma tell you to do. There are a lot of people who love you. Don't feel like you have to do everything by yourself. It will be a while before I come home, but when I return we will be a family again.

Love,
Momma

P.S. I love your drawing

Dr. Brown said that in order to get things out, you can also write or draw. Rocky wrote his mother a letter, and he really shared how he felt in the past and how he was currently feeling. He even drew a picture. Rocky's mom wrote back.

Grandma helped him with his homework at night, and they would talk about his feelings. Rocky remembered the good times he and his mother shared. Sometimes he would cry, but it was okay now. He wasn't quite as angry anymore. They made plans for when mom would come home. Everybody decided that once she returned, they would continue counseling as a family.

Rocky hoped that the next two years would pass by really fast. With everybody's help, he knew he could make it.

Our faces can show how we feel.

Draw a picture to express how you are feeling.

Write a letter to your parent and tell them how you feel.

_____

_____

_____

_____

Dear _____:

I am feeling _____

_____.

I hope that _____

_____

Love,

_____

P.S. _____

To the Reader:

Rocky faced a number of challenges in his life, but he learned how to overcome them. We are sure that there are a lot of kids like Rocky out there. If you enjoyed reading about "Rocky", please send us your questions and comments. The authors are also available for speaking engagements and may be contacted at the following email addresses:

Dr. Janice Beal
bealcounseling@gmail.com

Judge Vanessa Gilmore
www.vanessadgilmore.com

Printed in the United States
by Baker & Taylor Publisher Services